This book is for all the little boys and girls that feel unseen in this world. I see you and you are beautiful!

To my two monsters:
Jaylen, you are forever my one and only "unofficial book club buddy".
Ty, you will ALWAYS be my bacon!

Nothing in this world makes me happier than watching you two smile and laugh with each other.
I Love you MORE!!!

Written by Shannon C. Singleton
Illustrated by Ujala Shahid
Edited and book designed by Bryony van der Merwe

Published in 2024
by I Rise Publishing

I RISE
PUBLISHING

ISBN: 979-8-9900501-1-2

Jaylen & Ty's Adventures
Based on True Stories

TICKLE ME
MOMMY!

Shannon C. Singleton

Illustrated by Ujala Shahid

I Rise Publishing

On a warm spring **Saturday,**

Jaylen was in the mood to **play.**

He zipped through the house with a **zoom,**

until he found Mom in the laundry **room.**

"Tickle me, Mommy!" Jaylen exclaimed. "Tickle me on my **toes,**

or how about my **nose?** Tickle me, Mommy, tickle me!"

Mom said, "Jaylen, I can't, not **yet.**
I haven't finished washing.

And I also need to fold
what's in the **basket.**"

Jaylen was really
sad that they
couldn't **play.**

"Mom, I can help,
things will go
faster that **way.**"

"Jaylen, thanks for the offer. That's very kind of **you.**

But you're not quite old enough for me to teach you what to **do.**"

Later, when Mom was finished with the clothes, Jaylen walked up to her and begged,

"Tickle me, Mommy, on my **thighs.**
Please tickle me under my **eyes!**"

Mom smiled and replied, "Sorry, honey, I don't have time **yet.** I have to finish cooking. We'll do it later, I won't **forget.**"

Jaylen's smile faded and he hung his head **low.**

He mumbled, "Okay," and walked away, real **slow.**

A good while passed, it was now **afternoon,**

when Jaylen came out of the living **room.**

He found Mom searching in the laundry **room.** She peeped into the closet and said, "I'm looking for the **vacuum.**"

"I can help.
I know what to **do.**

I'll look everywhere
and find it for **you.**"

"And after, you can tickle me, Mommy, on my **back,**

or under my feet.
You know I'd REALLY like **that!"**

"I can't," Mom said sadly.
"We'll have fun soon, don't **fret.**

I just haven't finished cleaning up.
Why don't you go play with your toy **jet?"**

Quietly, Jaylen went to his
room and did as he was **told.**

He whizzed around with
his toy jet but this soon got **old.**

Later, Mom was giving him a bath.
"Tickle me on my ear or maybe my **neck!**"

She replied with a soft chuckle,
"Not right now, not while you're **wet.**"

Jaylen's smile turned into a frown.
He thought, "We're never going to **play!**

It's just not fair. Why is Mom so
busy **today?"**

Then it was evening. Jaylen sat watching TV on the **couch.**

Mom crept up slowly from behind, and then pounced with a **shout!**

She tickled
his **toes**

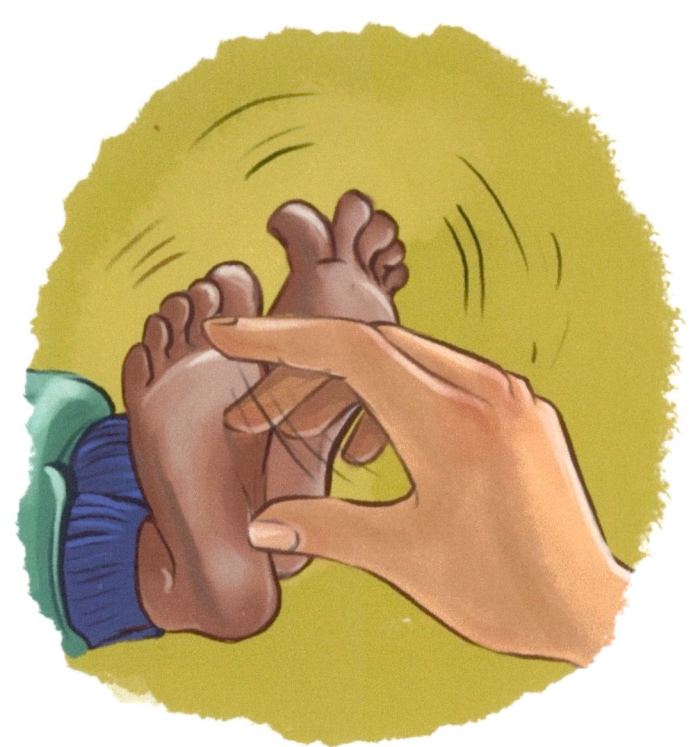

and all around
his **nose!**

She tickled
his **thighs**

and under
his **eyes!**

But Mom wasn't finished
with her surprise **attack.**

She tickled him under his feet
and all over his **back!**

She didn't leave any place
on his list **unchecked.**

She even tickled his ears
and his **neck!**

Jaylen laughed and laughed
until he almost ran out of **air.**

He couldn't tell how long
they'd been playing **there.**

He had such a good time. He said, "This is the greatest tickle **yet.** Next time I ask, I know Mommy won't **forget!**"

The Real Jaylen

Jaylen at 4 years old

Keep the Laughter Going!

Bring Tickle Me Mommy! to life with FREE guided lesson plans, printable activities, and complete Kindergarten, 1st Grade, and 2nd Grade curriculum. Designed for families and classrooms, these ready-to-use resources turn giggles into meaningful learning and help extend the story beyond the final page.

Scan the QR code below to get instant access!

subscribepage.io/ZlO13L

Other Works by This Author

Jaylen & Ty's Adventures series

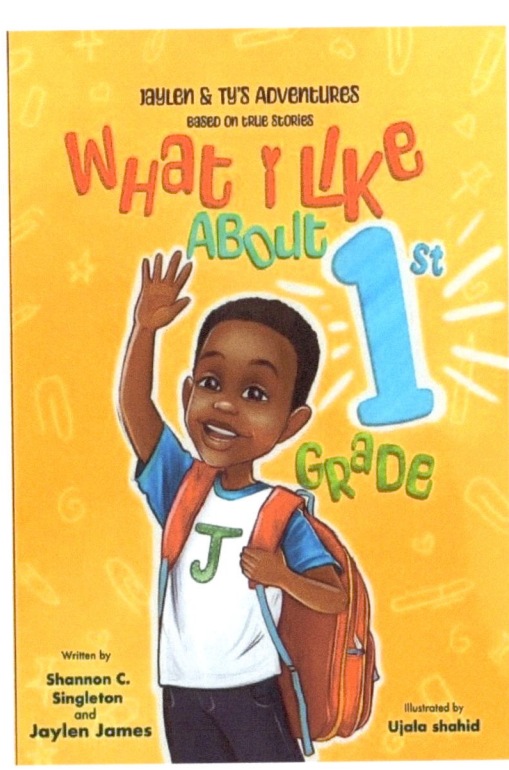

To learn more about each book, use the link
or QR Code below.

https://www.irisepublishing.com/books/jaylen-tys-adventures-series

 # About the Author

Shannon Singleton has been mesmerized by books ever since she was able to read. Her fascination with them led to her love of writing when she took Mrs. Tureau's creative writing class in 7th grade.

She is the mother of two sons, Jaylen and Ty. From a young age, Jaylen also shared her passion for reading. His ability to devour books within a day or two was amazing! Through his reading, Jaylen quickly found there weren't many books available with African American protagonists as the main character or any black characters at all. Jaylen did not see himself in the books he read.

This is something Shannon also experienced. Due to this and other events, Shannon decided to be the change she wanted to see and wrote her own book series!

She hopes that the Jaylen and Ty's Adventures Based on True Stories series allows black boys and girls to see themselves represented in a positive way really early in their lives and also for the world to see them for who they truly are!

To learn more about Shannon use the link or QR codes below.
https://www.irisepublishing.com/meet-our-authors/shannon-c-singleton

Facebook

Instagram

@SHANNONCSINGLETON_AUTHOR

A Word From the Author

I appreciate you taking the time to read my book with your little one (or by yourself - no judgment here! 🙃). If you enjoyed this book, it would mean a lot to me if you took a few minutes to leave a genuine review on the platform you purchased it from. Your thoughtful feedback is very important. Thank you for your time and support!

Shannon C. Singleton

www.ingramcontent.com/pod-product-compliance
Lightning Source LLC
Chambersburg PA
CBHW041452120626
46547CB00002B/424